A Trevor Wye
Practice Book for the
Flute
Volume 2
Technique

Order No: NOV 120522

NOVELLO PUBLISHING LIMITED
8/9 Frith Street, London W1V 5TZ

FOR MICKY

CONTENTS

		page
Preface		4
TECHNIQUE—General		5
(a)	Daily Exercises—I	7
(b)	Daily Exercises—II	10
(c)	Scale Exercises	13
(d)	Machiavellian Exercises—I	26
(e)	Machiavellian Exercises—II	28
RELAXING		30
TRILLS		30
SEQUENCES		33
EXAMPLES		39

A PREFACE TO BE READ

TO THE STUDENT

This book is about practising; how to extract the most from it, how to be more efficient at it and how to isolate and overcome some of the difficulties of the flute. It is by no means intended to be definitive. It was written to help you achieve good results with many of the flute problems, in the shortest time.

If the exercises are practised properly, it will shorten the time spent on the building blocks of flute playing, and so allow more time for music making.

These points about practising in general, are important:

(a) Practise the flute only because you *want* to; if you don't want to – don't! It is almost useless to spend your allocated practice time wishing that you weren't practising.

(b) Having *decided* to practise, make it difficult. Like a pest inspector, examine every corner of your tone and technique for flaws and practise to remove them. Only by this method will you improve quickly. After glancing through this book, you will see that many of the exercises are simply a way of looking at the same problem from different angles. You will not find it difficult to invent new ways.

(c) Try always to practise what you *can't* play. Don't indulge in too much self-flattery by playing through what you can already do well.

(d) As many of the exercises are taxing, be sure your posture and hand positions are correct. It is important to consult a good teacher on these points (see page 9 in Practice Book VI—ADVANCED PRACTICE).

GUARANTEE

Possession of this book is no guarantee that you will improve on the flute; there is no magic in the printed paper. But, if you have the desire to play well and put in some reasonable practice, you cannot fail to improve. It is simply a question of *time*, *patience* and *intelligent work*. The book is designed to avoid unnecessary practice. It is concentrated stuff. *Provided* that you follow the instructions carefully, you should make more than twice the improvement in half the time! *That is the guarantee.*

TO THE TEACHER

This is one of a series of basic exercise books for players of all ages who have been learning from about a year up to and including students at music colleges and universities. There are some recommended speeds, but these should be chosen to accommodate the ability of the player. Some exercises are more difficult than others: take what you feel your students need.

TREVOR WYE 1979

TECHNIQUE—GENERAL

Regular practice is most important to progress in technique. Time lost cannot be made up the next day. If an athlete misses two days of training, he doesn't try, in one day, to make up for all the time he has lost. He would soon pull a muscle.

Work *regularly* at technique.

Work for longer at the keys you find most difficult.

Whatever time is available to you for practice, about one third should be spent on these exercises.

Work hardest at the weakest fingers.

When a difficulty arises, repeat the difficult bar *four more times*.

In all the exercises:—

(a) maintain a good posture. Never sit down.

(b) use a good tone.

(c) play with clockwork precision.

(d) try to keep your fingers close to the keys.

It cannot be too strongly emphasised that technical progress is a question of *time, patience* and *intelligent work*.

TECHNIQUE

The finger muscles need constant practice to achieve (a) independence from each other and (b) speed. Scales are essential to this aim, but *only* when played from the tonic or keynote to the top of the compass, then down to the lowest note on the flute and back again to the keynote:

One-octave scales, or scales over a twelfth, are not much good; your time would more profitably be spent elsewhere. Scales over the whole compass, *played slowly*, are within the reach of most young players. True, most local examinations require scales over one octave or a twelfth. This is to keep in line with all the other instruments. The flute fingering is easier than the clarinet, oboe and bassoon and it is easier to play fast in all keys on the flute. Therefore you should aim at the ideal of exercising your fingers and brain over the whole range of the flute from low C to high B *in all keys*. In preparation for these scales, therefore, the following exercises are important. Before starting, it would be a good plan to exercise the weakest fingers—the right hand third finger and little finger—and to stretch the little finger so that low C sharp and C natural can be played without it straightening. *Always bend the little finger*. If necessary, use it on its *right* side. Play this exercise using the little finger on the C sharp *key* —the one with the pad in—to play C sharp! *Try not to move your hand.*

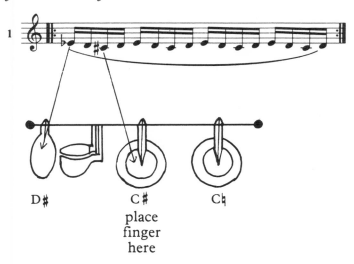

D♯   C♯   C♮

place
finger
here

6

Repeat this exercise many times during your practice. Then change the E flat to an E natural but *make sure you use your D sharp key for E natural!*
Remember, too, to slide your little finger when required. Rub the tip of your little finger along the side of your nose; it will gather skin oil and will slide on the keys more easily.

Here are some more:

Repeat the above with C sharp instead of C natural.

Don't try to do all these exercises in one day. Rather work at them over the course of a month or more and return to them when you need to.

You should feel a distinct fatigue in the hands after playing them, but don't practise any more after *pain* is felt.

Also see the section on relaxing.

Now commence the Daily Exercises I remembering the following points:

(a) strive for evenness; play like clockwork.
(b) always use the 'correct' fingering, i.e. (1) middle E flat with first finger off; (2) F sharp always with third finger right hand; (3) use D sharp key for every note except low and middle D natural (and low C natural and C sharp) and the very top B natural and C.
(c) always use the most difficult fingering, i.e. B flat with the first finger of the right hand. *See preface, note (b)*
(d) play the exercises with a *good tone*.
(e) practise them every day.

PROBLEMS BOX

When you have difficulty playing—with the correct fingering!—two or three notes together, then the numbers at the end of each line refer to the Scale Exercises which follow; these will help you overcome your particular problem. After a time, it will no longer be necessary to refer to these exercises as they are quite self-explanatory. They back up points (b) and (c) in the preface.

DAILY EXERCISES—I

MAJOR

See previous exercises for little finger Nos. 2, 3, 4

See previous ex. No. 5

See Nos. 6, 7, 8

8

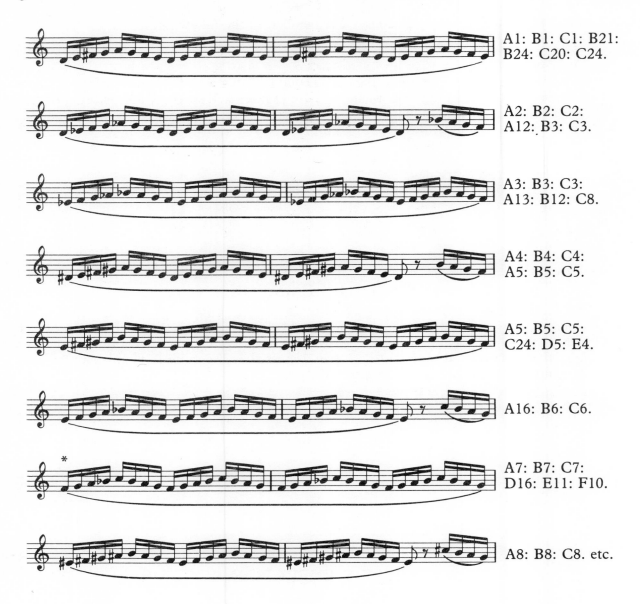

A1: B1: C1: B21: B24: C20: C24.

A2: B2: C2: A12: B3: C3.

A3: B3: C3: A13: B12: C8.

A4: B4: C4: A5: B5: C5.

A5: B5: C5: C24: D5: E4.

A16: B6: C6.

A7: B7: C7: D16: E11: F10.

A8: B8: C8. etc.

By referring to the Scale Exercises, it will be clear how to work at the remainder of the Daily Exercises and will help you to invent new ways of overcoming your technical problems. Write in the scale exercise numbers yourself in the right-hand column if you wish.

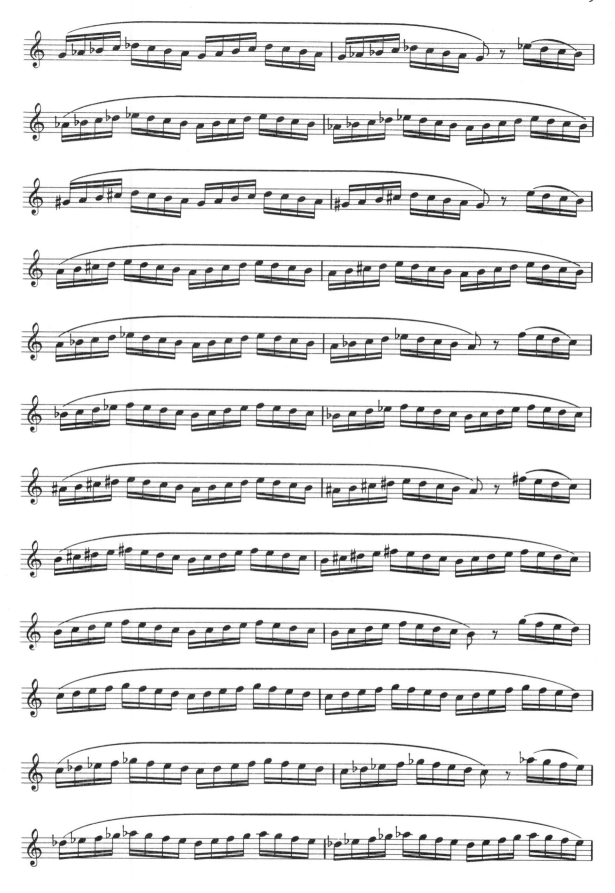

Be sure to finger E flat with the first finger off, and use the D sharp key for E natural. In case of difficulty, some E flat exercises can be found in VOL. III—ARTICULATION.

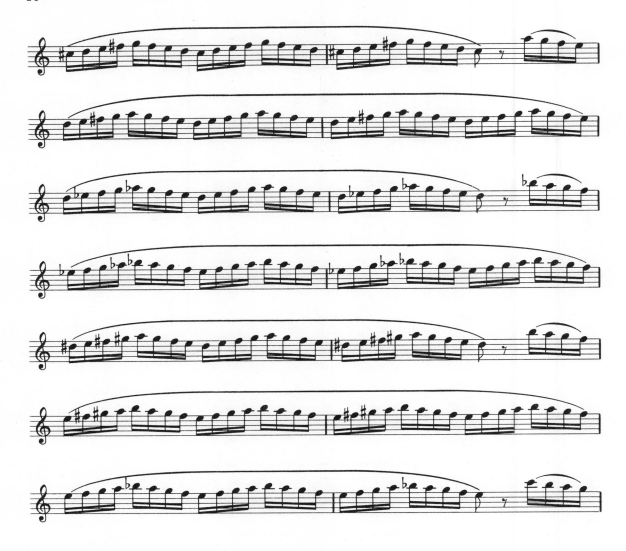

Now go back to the sign ★ and continue one octave higher as far as you can. If your familiarity with the upper register is limited, try to include one *new* line each week. You will soon reach all the upper notes.

DAILY EXERCISES—II

MINOR

Be sure to finger E flat with the first finger off, and use the D sharp key for E natural. In case of difficulty, some E flat exercises can be found in VOL. III—ARTICULATION.

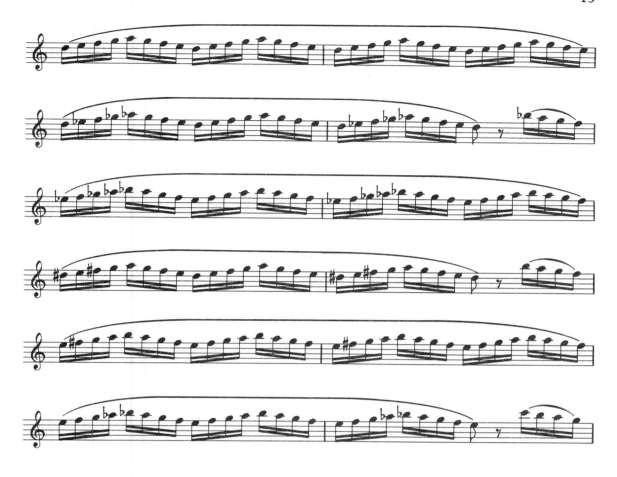

Now go back to the sign ＊ and continue one octave higher as far as you can. If your familiarity with the upper register is limited, try to include one *new* line each week. You will soon reach all the upper notes.

PROBLEM BOX

Where any unevenness or difficulty occurs, remember to use the appropriate Scale Exercises to help isolate and overcome the problem. See preface note (c).

SCALE EXERCISES

Perhaps, so far, you have used these scale exercises only as a remedy for technical difficulties in the Daily Exercises. If so, now practise them as exercises in their own right. They are most valuable. DON'T GET DISHEARTENED. Remember that these are CONCENTRATED exercises. You will achieve much quicker technical results with these studies than in books full of pretty Victorian studies.

Keep at them!

SCALE EXERCISES

SERIES A: MAJOR

Repeat the whole one octave higher and then two octaves higher as far as No. 7. Be sure to finger E flat with the first finger off, and use the D sharp key for E natural. In case of difficulty, some E flat exercises can be found in VOL. III—ARTICULATION.

SERIES B: MAJOR

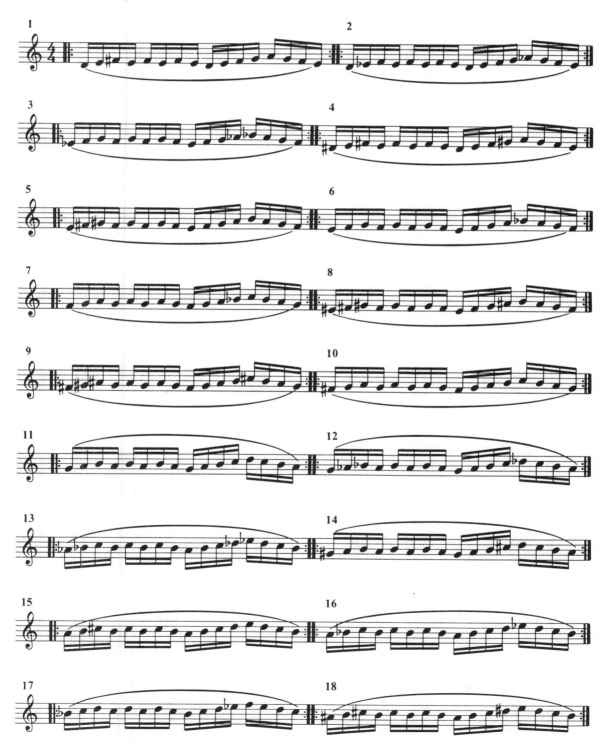

16

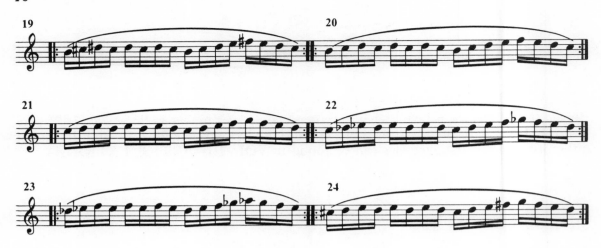

Repeat the whole one octave higher and then two octaves higher as far as No. 7. Be sure to finger E flat with the first finger off, and use the D sharp key for E natural. In case of difficulty, some E flat exercises can be found in VOL. III—ARTICULATION.

SERIES C: MAJOR

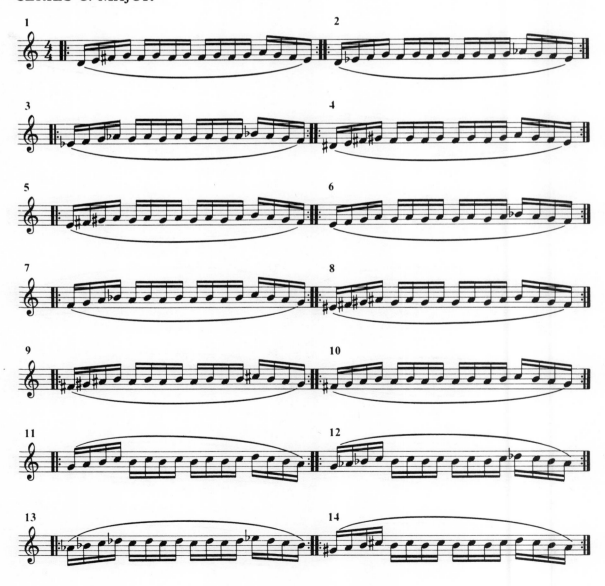

Repeat the whole one octave higher and then two octaves higher as far as No. 7.

SERIES D: MINOR

18

Repeat the whole one octave higher and then two octaves higher as far as No. 7. Be sure to finger E flat with the first finger off, and use the D sharp key for E natural. In case of difficulty, some E flat exercises can be found in VOL. III—ARTICULATION.

SERIES E: MINOR

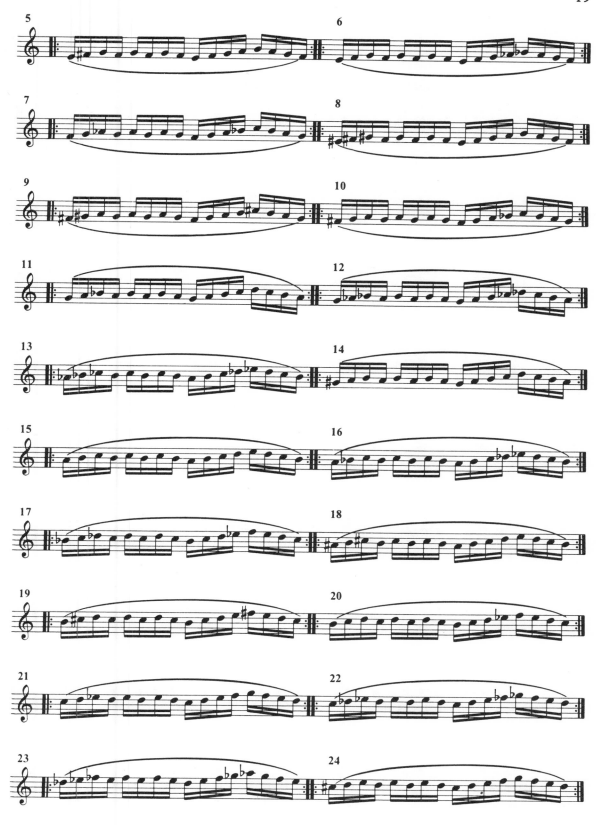

Repeat the whole one octave higher and then two octaves higher as far as No. 7.

20

SERIES F: MINOR

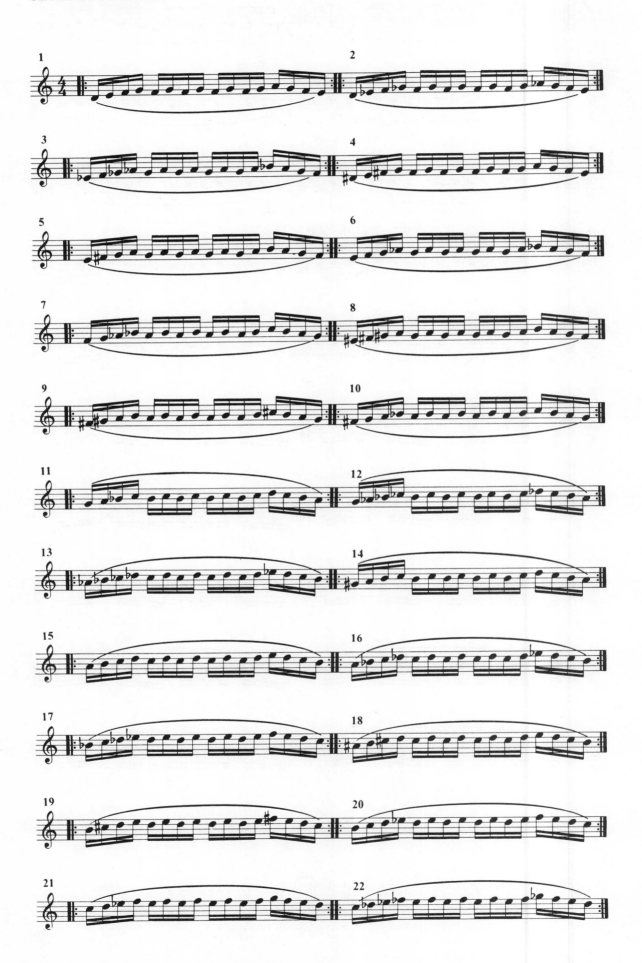

Repeat the whole exercise one octave higher and then two octaves higher as far as No. 7.

DAILY EXERCISES—II

Practise these exercises *every day*. A short period every day *will* achieve results. Once a week at them will not. Unless you intend to live as long as Methuselah: he lived 969 years.

MAJOR

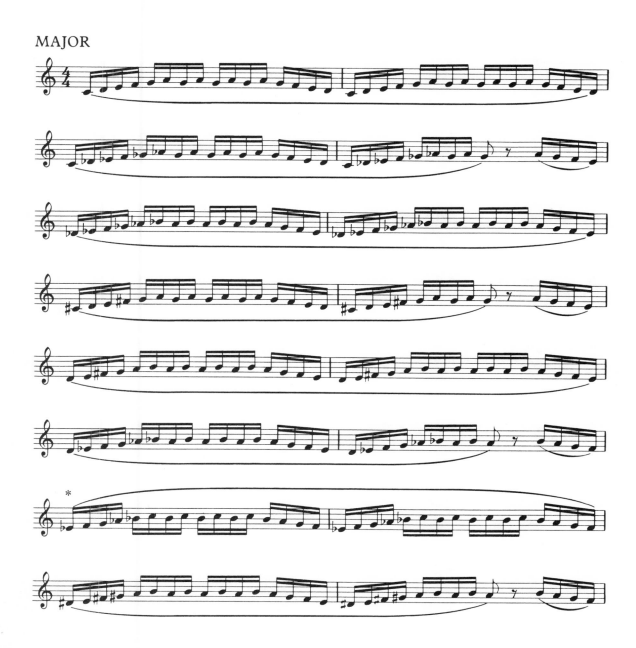

22

Go back to the sign ★ and repeat one octave higher to the end.

MINOR

24

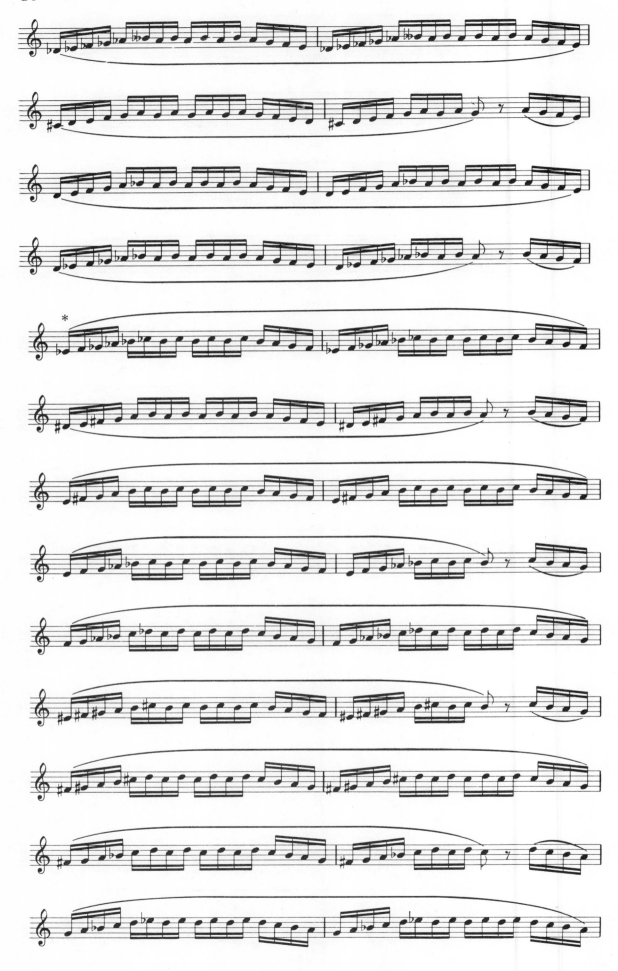

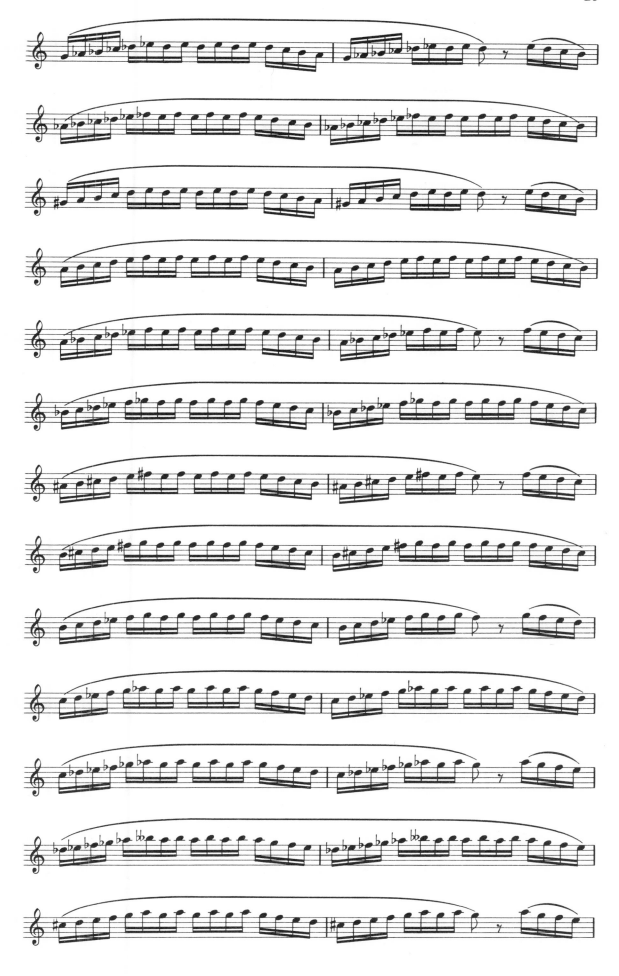

25

26

Go back to the sign ★ and repeat one octave higher to the end.

MACHIAVELLIAN EXERCISES*

These two exercises are difficult. However, following your acceptance of the preface—(b) and (c)—take pleasure in the difficulties encountered.

The Machiavellian exercises are hard, but do remember that it is really concentrated stuff. You will find just *one* of these bars wrapped up in many a pretty nineteenth-century study. But the practice—and the mastery—of that one bar was really the point of the whole study!

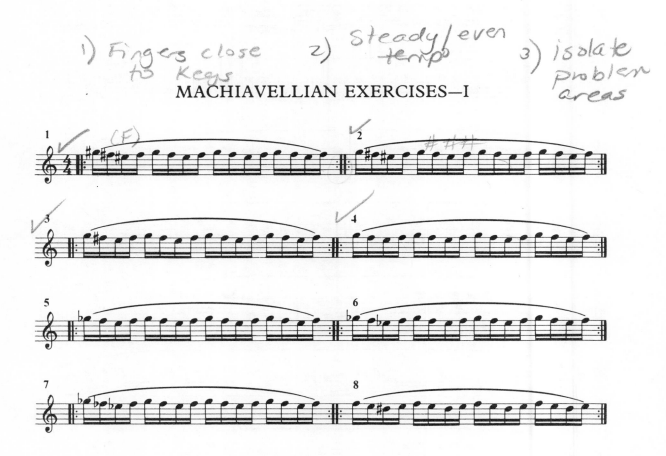

*Machiavelli (1469-1527): A Florentine statesman who had a reputation for craftiness and guile.

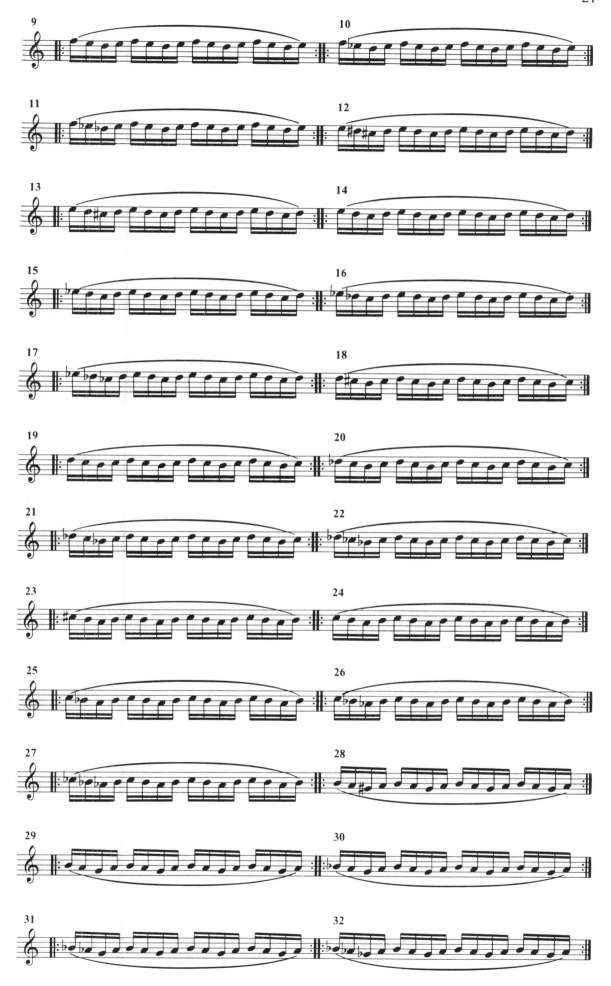

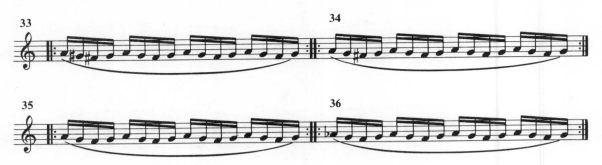

Repeat Nos. 1-20 one octave higher. Be sure to finger E flat with the first finger off, and use the D sharp key for E natural. In case of difficulty, some E flat exercises can be found in VOL. III—ARTICULATION.

Now repeat the exercise as a *continuous* study; i.e. without repeating each bar.

MACHIAVELLIAN EXERCISES—II

MACHIAVELLIAN EXERCISES—II is more difficult, but it *can* be fun. Roll your sleeves up and go to it, but always remember to practise it with:—
(a) clockwork evenness
(b) correct fingering
(c) good tone.

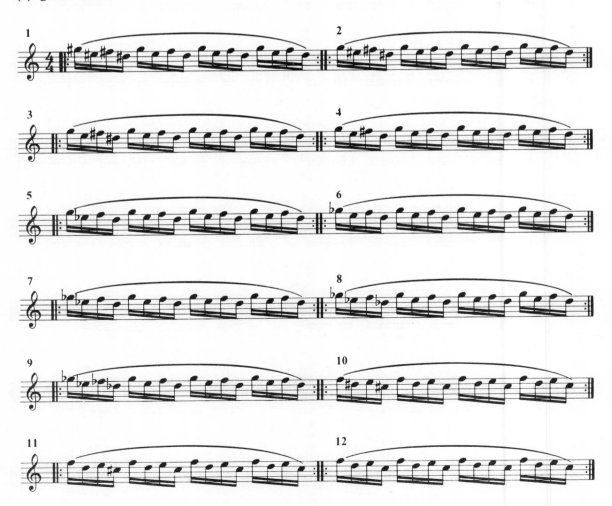

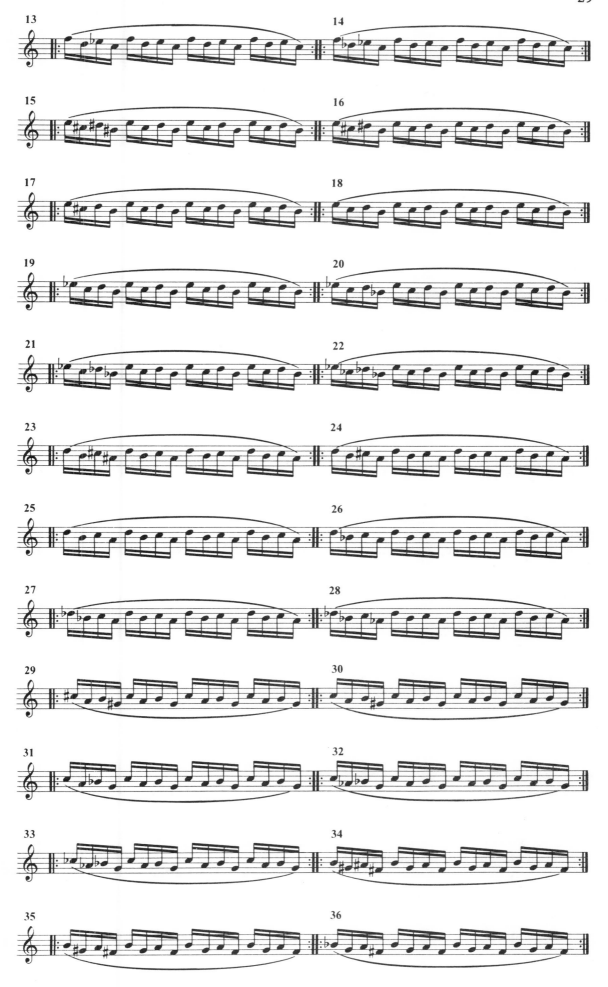

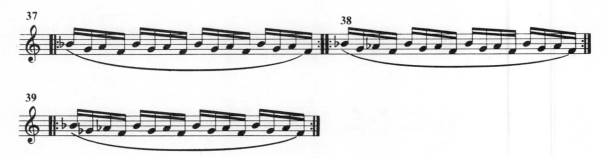

Repeat Nos. 1-26 one octave higher.

Technique: examples of difficult passages abound; you will find three examples at the end of the book.

Now repeat the exercise as a *continuous* study; i.e. without repeating each bar.

RELAXING

Choose some paperback books of the same thickness as the width of your hand. Lie down on the floor with knees raised and slightly apart. Place the books under your head with hands and arms to the side. You will notice an arch in the small of the back; this will gradually disappear. It usually takes about five minutes to assume contact with the floor. As it does you will feel your spine becoming a little longer and will probably want to move your hips down a little. Remain like this for at least ten minutes.
This relaxing position is used by many artists, both actors and musicians to loosen up and relax before going on stage.
When undergoing long tiring hours of instrumental practice, you will find it helpful to relax both during and after these sessions. It is particularly useful to counteract the tensions which can result when practising technically difficult studies such as the exercises for low C sharp and the little finger of the right hand, and the Machiavellian Exercises.

TRILLS

Most players avoid trill studies. They are difficult but *most important* for the development of a fine technique.
Before commencing, note carefully the following points:
(a) even when playing slowly, move the finger *quickly* up and down. Pat the keys going down and pat the air coming up!
(b) be *really* rhythmic in this exercise. Play exactly the right number of notes in the right time.
(c) always make a good tone on *both* notes when trilling, especially when using the trill keys or other 'weak' notes. See also VOL. I—TONE.
(d) don't move the *hand* whilst trilling. *See preface, note (d)*

EXAMPLE

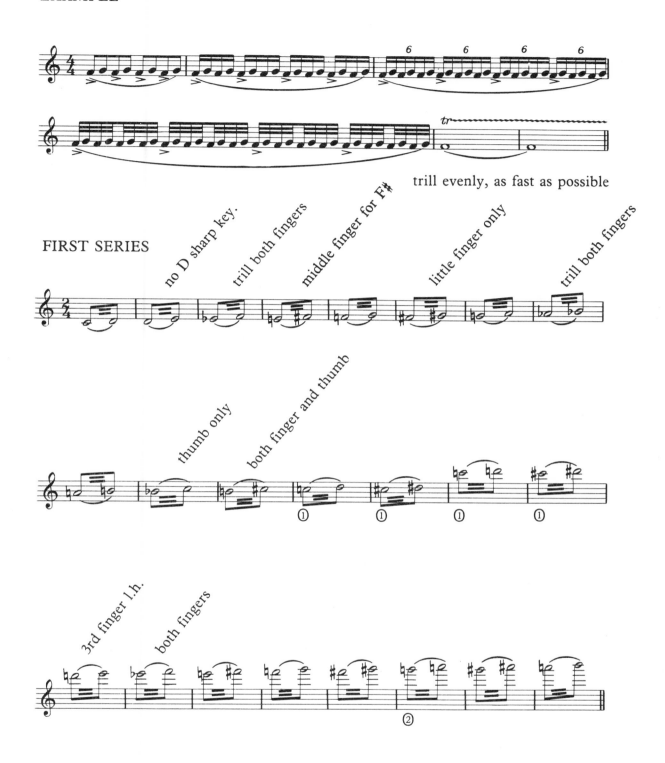

trill evenly, as fast as possible

FIRST SERIES

①Check these trills in the trill exercises found in VOL. 1—TONE.

②If you can't find a satisfactory trill for this note, finger top G natural and trill the first finger of the left hand and the first trill key *alternately*.
Practise it; it really works!

SECOND SERIES

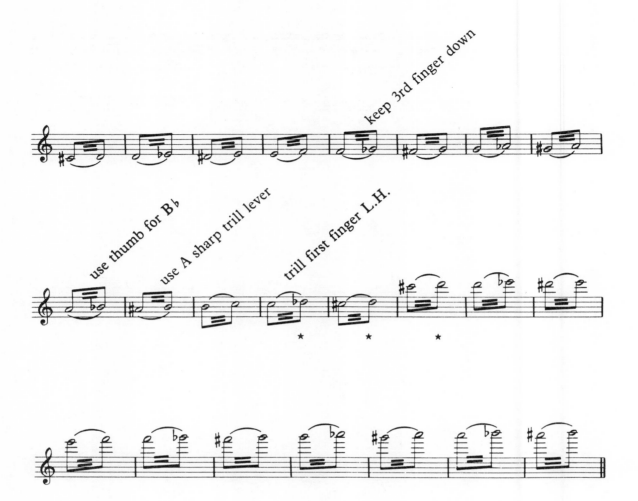

┌───┐

PROBLEM BOX

If any discomfort is felt in wrist, arm, shoulder or neck whilst practising trill exercises, consult your teacher regarding posture. Also try the relaxing exercise.

└───┘

*Exercises for the *tone* of trills and for C sharp can be found in VOL. I – TONE, on p.37.

SEQUENCES

These exercises help sight-reading, improvisation, the reflexes and your memory. The problem we all find with sight-reading is not so much not being able to play the notes, but responding *quickly* enough to the written notes, especially if there are some difficult accidentals!

These sequences will also enable those who are keen on baroque music or jazz to get to know the flute well enough to be able to improvise – a most useful accomplishment and one to which many an orchestral player has had to resort when he has lost his place!

Play through this first exercise. Later, try not to read the notes; play from memory if you can. If you aren't very familiar with the extreme top of the compass, find the way to come down with elegance. Like a mountain, go up only as far as you can!

More exercises for improvisation can be found in VOL. 5 – BREATHING AND SCALES.

MAJOR

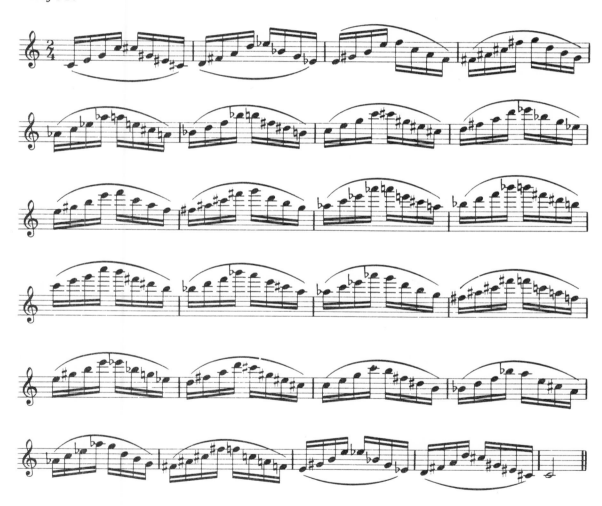

Now practise the same exercise again with these different rhythms:

34

The minor form is not so easy and may take a little longer to master:

MINOR

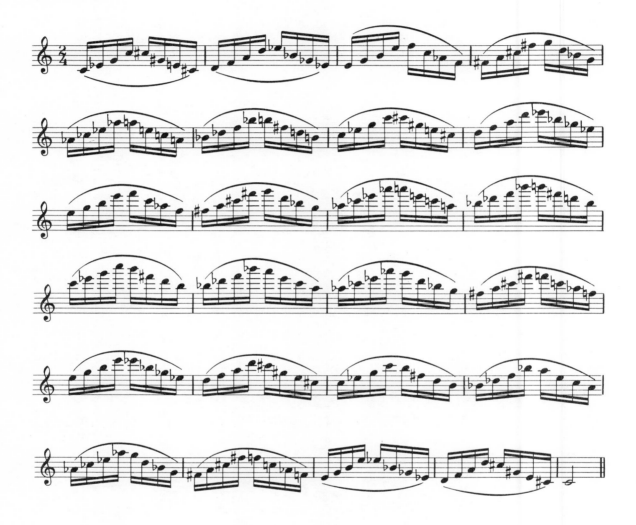

Sequences are like stairs; they can go up and down in sequence or in double sequence. In other words, they can be made to go three steps up and one step down. But, of course, they have to be played fast enough to appreciate the pattern.

etc.

Here are some others. When the rhythm is changed, the possibilities are endless.

DOMINANT SEVENTHS

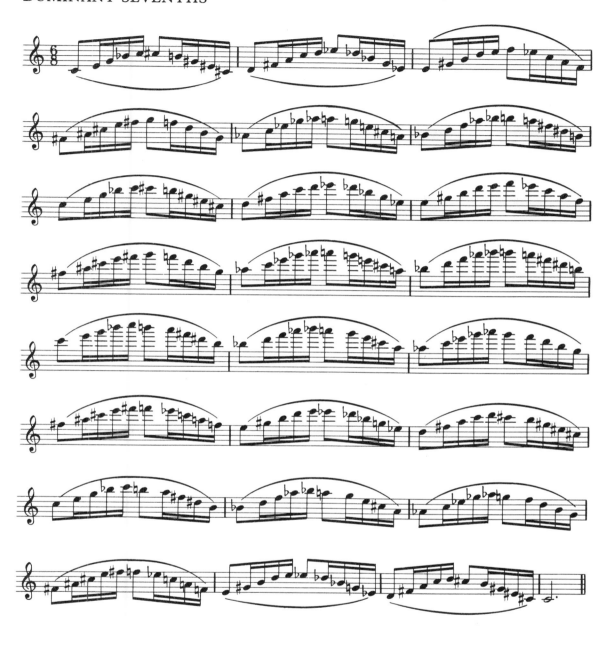

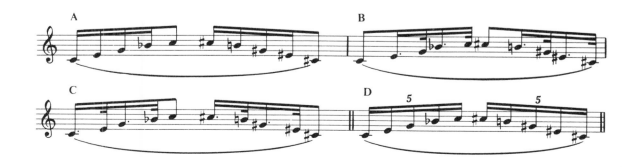

36

Here are some more ideas or variants:

MAJOR

or perhaps you would prefer a few slinky ones like:

or

DIMINISHED TRIADS

Diminished triads are very beautiful and as there are only three groups of different notes, they are somewhat easier to remember:

and

and

and, of course

and therefore

The scale sequences which follow are not easy but are still a most valuable form of practice:

MAJOR

etc.

etc.

MINOR

etc.

etc.

Some examples of the use of sequences can be found at the end of this book.

EXAMPLES

Here are some extracts from the flute repertoire which illustrate the various points raised in this book.

TECHNIQUE

ST JOHN PASSION

J. S. BACH

No. 25

SYMPHONIA DOMESTICA

R. STRAUSS[1]

Scherzo

TILL EULENSPIEGEL

R. STRAUSS[2]

TRILLS

SYMPHONY NO. 5

SHOSTAKOVICH

IL PENSIEROSO

HANDEL

VARIATIONS ON A THEME OF ROSSINI CHOPIN

CHANSON D'AMORE DOPPLER

SONATINE DUTILLEUX[3]

SUITE B. GODARD

GODARD: this often causes the young player to stumble at this point:

How grand this ending sounds! The trills add such excitement to the final bars of this solo:

SEQUENCES

CONCERTO IN G   C. P. E. BACH

AIRS VALAQUES   DOPPLER

etc.

FANTASIE PASTORALE HONGROISE DOPPLER

CANTABILE E PRESTO ENESCO[4]

PIECE IBERT[5]

[4]Reproduced by permission of Enoch et Cie—Paris, U.K. and Commonwealth agents Edwin Ashdown Ltd.
[5]Copyright by Alphonse Leduc & Cie Paris. Owners and publishers for all countries.

Printed and bound in Great Britain by
Halstan & Co. Ltd., Amersham, Bucks.

9/96 (25649)

A little humour goes a long way and without diminishing the importance of hard, dedicated work, Mr. Wye shows how enjoyable it can be—a most useful addition.

Peter Lloyd

I have read through your book with great interest and believe that it will form an important adjunct to the study and teaching material of the flute. It is just the sort of book which I would have liked to have produced myself. Congratulations on the book and best wishes for its success.

Geoffrey Gilbert

*This meets many of the very real problems of the flute in a way not set down in any other book. I shall recommend it to my pupils and shall not hesitate to recommend it to **you**.*

William Bennett

TREVOR WYE

VIDEO

PLAY THE FLUTE
A beginner's guide

TUTORS

A BEGINNER'S BOOK FOR THE FLUTE
Part 1
Part 2
Piano Accompaniment

PRACTICE BOOKS FOR THE FLUTE
VOLUME 1 Tone
(TONE CASSETTE available separately)
VOLUME 2 Technique
VOLUME 3 Articulation
VOLUME 4 Intonation and Vibrato
VOLUME 5 Breathing and Scales
VOLUME 6 Advanced Practice

A PICCOLO PRACTICE BOOK

PROPER FLUTE PLAYING

SOLO FLUTE

MUSIC FOR SOLO FLUTE

FLUTE & PIANO

A COUPERIN ALBUM
AN ELGAR FLUTE ALBUM
A FAURE FLUTE ALBUM
A RAMEAU ALBUM
A SATIE FLUTE ALBUM
A SCHUMANN FLUTE ALBUM
A VIVALDI ALBUM

A VERY EASY BAROQUE ALBUM, Vol. 1
A VERY EASY BAROQUE ALBUM, Vol. 2
A VERY EASY ROMANTIC ALBUM
A VERY EASY 20TH CENTURY ALBUM

A FIRST LATIN-AMERICAN FLUTE ALBUM
A SECOND LATIN-AMERICAN FLUTE ALBUM

MOZART FLUTE CONCERTO IN G K.313
MOZART FLUTE CONCERTO IN D K.314
AND ANDANTE IN C K.315

SCHUBERT THEME AND
VARIATIONS D 935 No. 3

FLUTE ENSEMBLE

THREE BRILLIANT SHOWPIECES